Visions et Propheties
Visions and Prophecies

Ernest Bloch

I

38987 c

T0050913

II

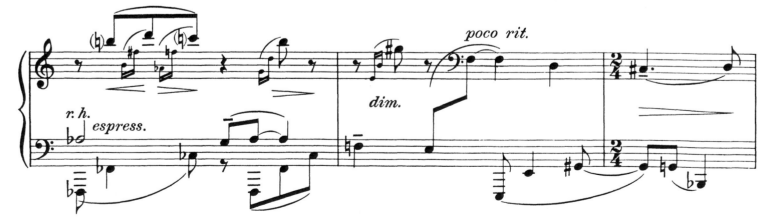

ERNEST BLOCH

VISIONS ET PROPHETIES

(Visions and Prophecies)

for the piano

G. SCHIRMER, Inc.

DISTRIBUTED BY

III

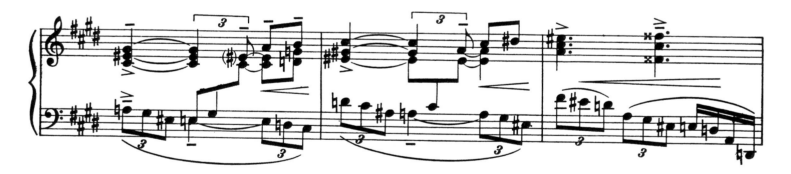

Poco più calmo ♩ = circa 76

a tempo poco più animato
♩ = 92 - 96

solenne

p sostenuto e marcato

poco a poco cresc.

mf

f ritmico

f ruvido

f

mf

f

molto ritmico

più f

p

accel.

ff a tempo

IV

Adagio, piacevole ♩ = circa 46

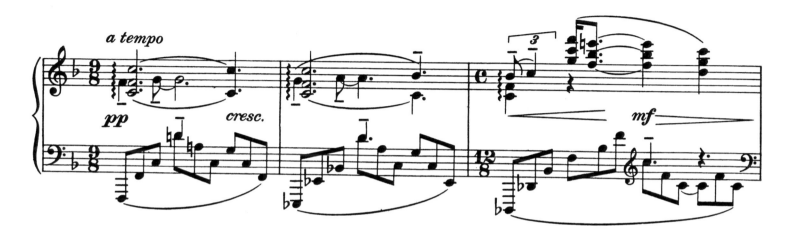

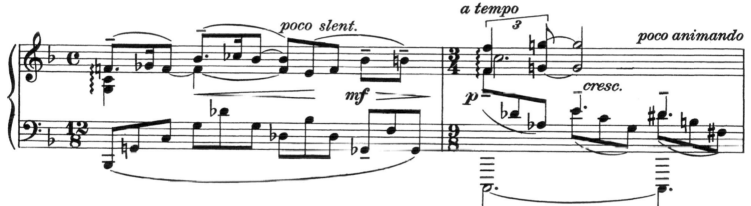

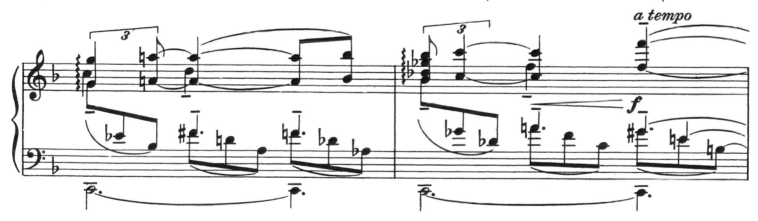

V

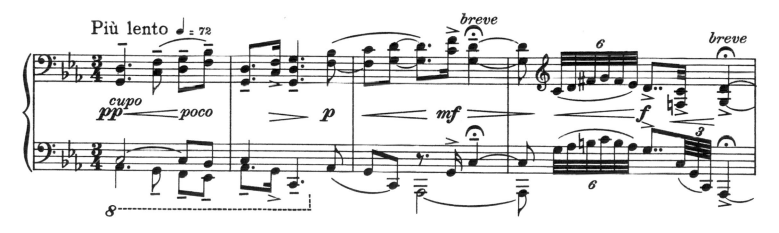

Agitando poco a poco
♩ = 84, *per cominciare, poi accelerando*

sempre agitando

♩ = 96

accel.

Poco meno mosso ed agitando ♩ = 84

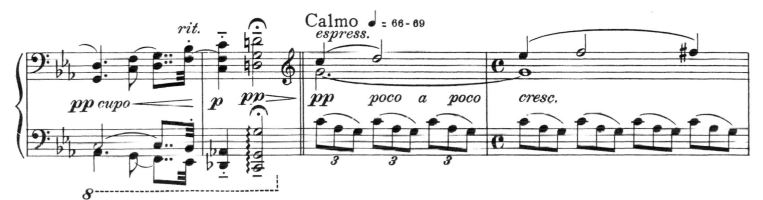

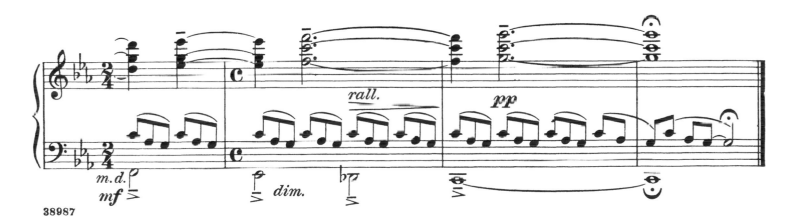

U.S. $7.95

HL50328750

G. SCHIRMER, Inc.

DISTRIBUTED BY

HAL•LEONARD®
CORPORATION

7777 W. BLUEMOUND RD. P.O. BOX 13819 MILWAUKEE, WI 53213

ISBN 978-0-7935-1587-5

CONCERTO for EUPHONIUM and Concert Band*

Robert Jager

Euphonium and Piano Reduction

*Concert Band or Symphony Orchestra
Accompaniments on rental

EDWARD B.
MARKS MUSIC
COMPANY

EXCLUSIVELY DISTRIBUTED BY
HAL•LEONARD®
CORPORATION
7777 W. BLUEMOUND RD. P.O. BOX 13819 MILWAUKEE, WI 53213